Disciplining

GROWING
GOD
IN

The Bible Study

JENNIFER N. PEARSON

First paperback edition January 2023

Cross image for cover and journal pages by Buckeye Design Company.

Interior layout and design by Delaney Medler

ISBN 978-1-7378811-4-8

CONTENTS

Dear Friends,

If you are reading this, then like me, your desire is to walk closer with Jesus daily. You long to hear from Him, and you are desperately looking for ways to rest in His promises. The truth is this: regardless of how close I may or may not be walking, my heart longs to be closer today than yesterday.

This Bible study is a journey. It is not intended to be a seven-week study that you complete, put on a shelf, and walk away from. Instead, this book is meant to bring you closer to God through the implementation of spiritual disciplines in your daily life.

Some of you just panicked when you read the word *discipline*—I know I did the first time. But believe me when I say that it is not what you are thinking or assuming. Disciplining yourself and your time for the purpose of growing closer to your Creator will refine and transform you in the best possible ways.

Among the many things God has revealed to me over the past several years is the importance of community. For this reason, I encourage you to go through this Bible study in a group setting. If you are not part of a group already, find one. If you cannot find one, start one. I can assure you that there are many others out there waiting for an invite to join you.

As you begin, please know that my prayer is that the tool you are holding in your hands will open your eyes to the goodness of God Almighty as you commit yourself and your time to growing in your knowledge and understanding of the One who called you according to His purposes.

Joyfully HIS,

Jennifer N. Pearson

Jennifer N. Pearson

Week 1

Introduction to Spiritual Disciplines

"Know that the LORD, he is God! It is he who made us, and we are his; we are his people, and the sheep of his pasture." Psalm 100:3

Can we just rest here for a moment? If you only read that verse above once, read it again—and again—and again. There is no better place to begin this study than acknowledging who God is. He is the One who created the universe and everything in it in six days and then rested on the seventh. He is the one whose plan was perfect from the beginning. And though sin and brokenness entered this perfect creation, His plan did not fail. He was not surprised, baffled, or taken aback. He is God. He is all-knowing and all-powerful. To Him there is no beginning and no end. And this mighty God brought us into this world as His children—His people. Just as sheep need the guidance and direction of their shepherd, so do we.

To that shepherd, every single sheep is equally important - so much so that if just one sheep were missing, he would leave the entire flock to find the one that had gone astray. And so our heavenly Father does for us. He loves us and longs for His child to be in right relationship with Him. What does it mean to be in a right relationship with God? First, we must acknowledge that He is God Almighty and every word written about Him in the Bible is completely accurate. This then leads us to recognize and understand our need for Him in our lives. After this, we must recognize that we are sinners in need of a Savior, confess and ask forgiveness for our sins, and surrender our life to Him by choosing to follow Him in obedience.

✓ Have you found salvation in Jesus Christ?

- No, but I am ready to! (Turn to page 72-73 and allow me to walk you through this.)
- Yes, I asked Jesus to be my Savior on the following date:_____

Many years ago, I read a book written by Donald S. Whitney that would change my walk with Jesus and my life forever in the best possible ways. In his book *Spiritual Disciplines for the Christian Life,* he said, "The Spiritual Disciplines are those practices found in Scripture that promote spiritual growth among believers in the gospel of Jesus Christ. They are the habits of devotion and experiential Christianity that have been practiced by the people of God since biblical times."[1] In other words, spiritual disciplines are ways that we devote ourselves and our time to God for the purpose of growing closer to Him. The result of this closeness is that by growing in our knowledge of Him we gain a deeper and better understanding of who He is and what He asks of His children.

✓ Without flipping through the book, list any spiritual disciplines that you are aware of.

_____

_____

_____

_____

✓ List which disciplines, if any, you have already implemented into your daily walk with the Lord.

_____

_____

_____

_____

_____

_____

_____

[1]Donald S. Whitney, Spiritual Disciplines for the Christian Life (Colorado Springs, CO: NavPress, 1991, 2014), 4.

✓ If you were able to write anything on the lines above, please take a minute and write out how these disciplines have impacted your life and your relationship with the one true God.

_____
_____
_____
_____
_____
_____
_____
_____
_____
_____
_____
_____
_____
_____
_____
_____
_____

For those who have walked this path for years, I pray that your walk is consistently deepened and that Christ reveals Himself to you through your active obedience to follow Him daily. And for those who feel as if these terms are foreign and a tad intimidating, just begin exactly where you are and allow the Holy Spirit to lead you down this path toward total reliance, dependence, and trust in Jesus Christ.

Complete Before Week 2 Meeting

☐ Answer all questions in this chapter.

☐ If you have not already, purchase your *Growing in God* journal, which is a necessary companion tool for this Bible study. (Available at www.joyfullyhis.org, Amazon.com, or any other major online bookstores.)

☐ Read pages 5-13 & 30-32 in your *Growing in God* journal. (If using the teen edition, read pages 1-10 & 39-41).

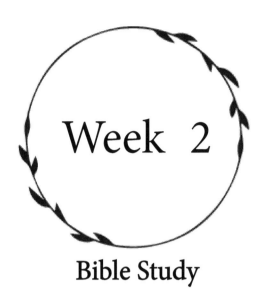

Week 2

Bible Study

✓ What does Bible Study look like for you currently?

_____

_____

✓ How often do you read your Bible?

_____

_____

This week is going to be about learning to implement Bible reading and study into your everyday life. While study in a group is beneficial to our spiritual growth, as followers of Christ it is imperative that we understand that Jesus must be our daily bread and our true source of fulfillment.

I believe so many people pick up the Bible to read and study God's Word and feel an overwhelming sense of intimidation. Most often, this feeling comes not from their lack of knowledge but instead from their confusion as to the best ways to read it. They look at the Bible as a whole, and it seems like a daunting task. Quite often, I'm approached with questions such as these: Where do I start reading? How much should I read at one time? What time of day should I read? What should I do when I don't understand what I read? This chapter is designed to offer answers and helpful tips to the questions above. In addition, we will examine some methods of reading the Bible in a manner that doesn't leave you feeling confused and overwhelmed.

Bible Reading Plans Options

Take some time to discuss the Bible reading options below as a group. Which ones have you attempted? Which ones have you found most beneficial to your daily walk? Which ways do you not prefer?

Cover to Cover: Reading the Bible as you would a regular book. This plan starts you at the very beginning and walks you all the way through the Bible from the beginning of the Bible (The Old Testament) to the end of the Bible (The New Testament).

Chronological: With this plan, you will read the Bible as the events happened historically. These plans are available on the Internet, a Bible app, and many other websites. In addition to this, you can also purchase chronological Bibles that allow you to read from beginning to end while still reading chronologically.

Individual books: This option allows you to pick any book of the Bible and read that book from beginning to end. For example, you might read and study the entire Book of Romans. Most likely, you would not read the whole book in one day but instead one chapter per day until you reach the end of the book.

Thematic or Topical: Different stages of our lives motivate us to dig deeper and develop our understanding on certain topics. You may be struggling with anxiety and in need some biblical wisdom to walk through the difficult days. Maybe you are engaged to be married and you are looking for biblical instruction on God's design for marriage. Or maybe you are a first time parent in need of guidance in this area. Regardless of which area of your life that you are seeking a better understanding, the Bible is our source of answers to all of life's questions. There are Bible reading plans for most any topic that you are in need of through a variaety of online sources as well as the Bible app.

Sectional: The Holy Bible is divided into two main parts: The Old Testament and The New testament. Within these parts there are 9 subparts. Knowing these divisions can help us to develop a reading plan where we read through each subpart or division separately. The Old Testament sections are the Law or also known as the Pentateuch, History, Poetry and Wisdom, Major Prophets, and Minor Prophets. The divisions of the New Testament are The Gospels, History, Letters or epistles, and Prophecy. On the following page you will find a chart that divides each book of the Bible into a section.

The Old Testament	
Law/Pentateuch	
Genesis	Numbers
Exodus	Deuteronomy
Leviticus	
History	
Joshua	2 Kings
Judges	1 Chronicles
Ruth	2 Chronicles
1 Samuel	Ezra
2 Samuel	Nehemiah
1 Kings	Esther
Poetry and Wisdom	
Job	
Psalms	
Proverbs	
Ecclesiastes	
Song of Songs	
Major Prophets	
Isaiah	Ezekial
Jeremiah	Daniel
Lamentations	
Minor Prophets	
Hosea	Nahum
Joel	Habakkuk
Amos	Zephaniah
Obdiah	Haggal
Jonah	Zechariah
Micah	Malachi

The New Testament	
The Gospels	
Matthew	John
Mark	
Luke	
History	
Acts	
Letters/Epistles	
Romans	Hebrews
1 Corinthians	James
2 Corinthians	1 Peter
Galatians	2 Peter
Ephesians	1 John
Phillippians	2 John
Colossians	3 John
1 Thessalonians	Jude
2 Thessalonians	
1 Timothy	
2 Timothy	
Titus	
Philemon	
Prophecy	
Revelation	

✓ List out other reading plans that you have tried:

_____

_____

✓ Have you ever read the entire Bible?

_____

✓ If yes, which plan did you use?

_____

✓ If no, what had hindered you from doing so?

_____

_____

While reading the Bible can definitely be a source of entertainment, its purpose is to be a tool of enlightenment, understanding and spiritual growth. Therefore, as we read, we should also study what we are reading for the purpose of gaining a deeper understanding of God's Word. As we read, there are methods we learn and apply that reveal to us the meaning and truths of the Bible. There is no set amount that you should read daily. It will differ from person to person. I would just like to encourage you to read for the purpose of gaining an accurate understanding versus reading for completion. Review and discuss the methods below as a group and compile a list of other methods you have used in your study time.

Bible Study Methods:

Sword Method: This study technique may seem simple, but it is quite powerful and has proven to be an extremely beneficial way to study the Bible.

How it works: As you are reading and studying, ask yourself four questions:

1. The blade tip of the sword points toward heaven: "What did this passage teach me about God?"

2. The sword handle is held by man: Ask yourself, "What does this passage say about man?"

3. The left blade: "Does this passage reveal a sin that should be avoided or a promise that we should be claiming?"

4. The right blade: Here we should ask ourselves what we learn from reading this passage regarding obedience to God. "Does this passage reveal an example to follow, or is there a command to obey?"

This method can be used with a single verse, several verses, or an entire passage. Lastly, ask yourself the following question: "How can I apply what I have learned to my life?" Using the explanation above, label the sword illustration on the following page by filling in the blanks.

The Sword Method

_____

Bible Character Study: With this study technique, you pick one major character from the Bible. Examples could include Adam, Abraham, Joseph, Moses, Peter, and so many more. We want to be careful not to mimic the behavior of these characters, because just like us, these Bible characters were flawed, sinful people as well. The Bible is not written to teach about the men and women in its pages; instead, it is written to teach about God in the lives of these people.

How it works: Pick a character from the Bible, and follow the steps below to learn more about this person.

1. Write down passages in which the Bible mentions this person.
2. List any character traits that become evident through your readings.
3. What lessons do you learn from reading the account of this person's life?
4. Have you walked through similar situations in your life?

Use the steps above to label the character on the following page with these steps.

Bible Character Study

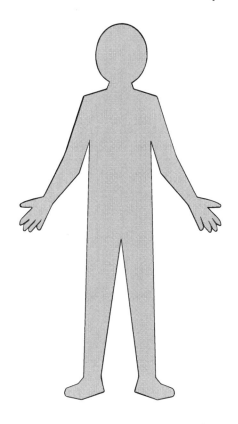

1. _____
   _____
2. _____
   _____
3. _____
   _____
   _____
   _____
4. _____
   _____
   _____
   _____
   _____
   _____

✓ As a group, make a list of other study methods you have used.

_____

_____

_____

_____

Application

This week, we are going to begin implementing Bible study as our first spiritual discipline into our daily life. The purpose of implementing one discipline at a time into your day is so that you can get a good grasp of one before adding another. Also, you will be doing this each day on your own and then coming together as a group to discuss the following week. I believe that studying in a group can be very beneficial to your spiritual growth, but our individual study is vital to our growth in Christ. As we read and study daily, we begin to understand that Jesus is our daily bread and our true source of fulfillment. As you begin to implement the spiritual discipline of Bible study, you will develop a dependence and a longing for this discipline in your daily life.

Over the following six weeks, you will commit yourself to reading and studying the Bible daily. I have provided a Bible reading plan that will walk you through the entire Book of John for the duration of this study. However, if you would like to create your own reading plan, please feel free to do so.

Complete Before Week 3 Meeting

☐ Read pages 14–18 in your *Growing in God* journal. (pages 11-16 if using the teen edition).

☐ Set a time daily that you will commit to reading your Bible.

☐ Decide on a quiet place where there will be no interruptions.

☐ Read week 1, days 1–7 in the reading plan found on the following page. Try not to cram all the days in at the end of the week. The purpose of this is to help you establish a daily routine of when and where you will read your Bible.

☐ Complete the remainder of this chapter before next week's meeting.

☐ Write out your daily Bible reading on your prayer journal pages in your *Growing in God* journal each day (p. 36 or p. 46 in teen edition). Once you have completed your reading, color in the circle next to "Bible study" on your calendar accountability page (p. 34 or p. 44 in teen edition).

☐ Be prepared to discuss what you have learned from this week's Bible reading during your next group meeting. Use the Notes section in your *Growing in God* journal, beginning on page 431 (p. 441 in teen edition).

Six-Week Bible Reading Plan on the Book of John

	Week 1	Week 2	Week 3	Week 4	Week 5	Week 6
Day 1	o 1:1-34	o 4:46-54	o 8:1-30	o 11:28-57	o 15: 1-17	o 18:25-40
Day 2	o 1:35-51	o 5:1-18	o 8:31-59	o 12:1-26	o 15:18-27	o 19:1-27
Day 3	o 2:1-12	o 5:19-47	o 9:1-12	o 12:27-50	o 16:1-15	o 19:28-42
Day 4	o 2:13-25	o 6:1-34	o 9:13-41	o 13:1-20	o 16:16-33	o 20:1-18
Day 5	o 3:1-21	o 6:35-71	o 10:1-21	o 13:21-38	o 17:1-19	o 20:19-31
Day 6	o 3:22-36	o 7:1-24	o 10:22-42	o 14:1-14	o 17:20-26	o 21:1-14
Day 7	o 4:1-45	o 7:25-53	o 11:1-27	o 14:15-31	o 18:1-24	o 21:15-25

The Sword Method

Complete the Sword Method by using John 1:1–5, or feel free to select your own verse or passage from the Book of John.

_____

_____

_____

_____

_____

_____   _____

_____   _____

_____   _____

_____   _____

_____   _____

_____   _____

_____   _____

_____

_____

_____

_____

The Character Method

Complete the Character Method by using the apostle John, or feel free to select your own character in the Book of John.

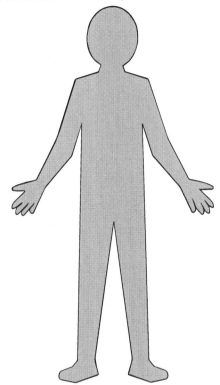

1. _____

_____

2. _____

_____

3. _____

_____

_____

_____

4. _____

_____

_____

_____

_____

_____

Week 3

Scripture Memorization and Meditation

† As a group, discuss some things that you learned from last week's Bible reading. In addition to this, discuss your answers on the sword method and character method and how they were helpful to you during your study time.

✓ Have you ever memorized Scripture?

_____

_____

✓ If yes, how did this help you grow as a follower of Christ?

_____

_____

_____

_____

_____

_____

✓ How long have you been memorizing Scripture?

_____

_____

✓ If not, what has hindered you from doing so?

_____

_____

_____

_____

This week, not only will we dig into how and why to memorize verses from the Bible, but we are also going to gain an understanding of what it means to meditate on the Word of God.

Scripture Memorization

Memorization is not a discipline that I implemented early in my life. However, once I began, it quickly became obvious to me how imperative it was for my growth in God. I cannot tell you the number of times that I would memorize a verse, and soon after the Holy Spirit would use that particular verse to speak directly to me as well as to others around me. Reading and studying the Bible are of absolute importance, but memorizing Scripture takes that knowledge one step further. It deepens our understanding and places it in our hearts and minds for the Lord to use for His purposes.

Scripture Memorization Methods

Read and Reread: This method of Scripture memorization is simple, easy, and can be done anywhere at any time. You start with a verse and read it several times to yourself. Continue reading the verse daily or even several times throughout the day until you have memorized it. Go back and review it often.

Listen: Some of us are better listeners than we are readers. If this is you, this method of listening to someone else say the verse will be helpful. Turn on an audio version of the Bible and listen to this verse throughout the day. Continue listening to it until you have it memorized. Go back often to review it.

✓ Do you find reading or listening more beneficial?

_____

_____

_____

Write It Out: This method is a tangible way to memorize Bible verses. Take a note card or a sticky note and write the verse on the item of your choice. Place it deliberately where it will grab your attention throughout the day.

Here are a few examples of my favorite spots to place my verses.

- Make it the screen saver of my phone.
- Place the sticky note on the edge of my computer screen.
- Use the card as a placeholder in my Bible.
- Place a dry erase board on my refrigerator and write the verse there.

✓ What are some other places that you can think of?

_____

_____

_____

Accountability: This method involves another person. The greatest part of this method is that two people (or more, if you choose) memorize Scripture at the same time. You read the verses together and make a plan to repeat them daily with one another. You don't move to the next verse until everyone in the group has memorized it. You intentionally plan review times each week to go over all the verses that you have memorized together.

✓ Who is a person or persons that you would like to have as a Scripture memorization accountability partner?

_____

_____

_____

Scripture Memorization Apps: This is one of my favorite methods. Most of us always have our phones with us, which makes this method very accessible. Most of us also have random ten-minute time increments in our day during which we can memorize a verse or do a quick review. My go-to app is BibleMemory. You can choose the lite version, which is free, or upgrade to the pro version. This app walks you through three different steps of memorization for each verse, and then it prompts you to review it often. Whether you are in the car line waiting to pick up your kids, finishing up your lunch break, or scrolling through your phone before bed, you can easily open the app and complete your daily memorization or review right from your phone or tablet.

✓ What are other apps that you know about or have used for Scripture memorization?

_____

_____

_____

✓ What are some other methods that you have used to memorize Scripture?

_____

_____

_____

I would encourage you to try out each method to see which one works for you. You can choose to use one or use them in combination with one another.

Scripture Meditation

Meditation can be thought of as a separate branch of Scripture memorization. Meditation can also be a helpful tool in memorization. When we memorize, we learn the verse and can recall it at any time. When we meditate on a verse, the outcome may be that we memorize it, but the purpose is to gain a deeper understanding of it. Meditation requires quiet alone time with God and His Word.

✓ Have you ever meditated on Bible verses?

_____

_____

Scripture Meditation Methods

Write it out in your own words. Use the Bible to examine what each word means. Make sure that you have a clear understanding of each word. Write out what that verse means to you.

Examine the verse. Ask yourself the following questions:
- Who wrote it?
- Who were they writing it to?
- When was it written?
- What was their purpose in writing it?
- What else did you learn from this verse?

Apply it to your own life. Read the verse and gain a clear understanding of it. Think of times in your life that this specific verse would have been helpful. In addition to this, think through ways that you can apply this verse to your daily life to help you grow closer to God in your walk and your obedience to Him.

✓ List additional methods that you know of or have used to meditate on verses in the Bible:

_____

_____

_____

_____

✓ For those of you who have practiced Scripture meditation before, how did it help you grow in your walk with God?

_____
_____
_____
_____
_____

✓ Which methods have you tried, and which one has proven to be the most helpful?

_____
_____
_____
_____
_____

Application

In addition to Bible study, this week we will be adding Scripture memorization and meditation to our daily time spent with God. I have listed several verses from the Book of John at the end of this chapter for you to memorize and meditate on. You can go through as many or as few as you would like. My suggestion would be to stay on a verse until you have memorized it fully and then move to the next one. Try out different methods to see which one is right for you. The next time your group meets, be prepared to recite one verse that you have memorized and share which method you used.

Complete Before Week 4 Meeting

☐ Read pages 19–22 in your *Growing in God* journal. (p. 17-25 if you are using the teen edition).

☐ Think through some times of your day during which you would like to practice memorizing Scripture.

☐ Pick a verse and begin memorizing it. (Sample verses on page 29-31).

☐ Decide on which method(s) you would like to try.

☐ As you memorize verses, write down the verses that you are memorizing in your *Growing in God* book on the daily prayer journal page. Once you have memorized the verse, write it in your *Growing in God* book on page 461(p.477 in teen edition).

☐ Color in the circle next to "Scripture memorization" on your accountability page for that month, just as you did for "Bible study."

☐ Be prepared to recite one verse that you memorized to your group.

☐ Choose a verse from John to meditate on.

☐ Read week 2, days 1–7 in your Bible reading plan.

☐ Write out your daily Bible reading on your prayer journal pages in your *Growing in God* journal each day (p. 36 or p. 46 in teen edition).Once you have completed your reading, color in the circle next to "Bible study" on your calendar accountability page (p. 34 or p. 44 in teen edition).

☐ Be prepared to discuss what you have learned from this week's Bible reading during your next group meeting. Use the Notes section in your *Growing in God* journal, beginning on page 431 (p. 441 in teen edition).

☐ Complete the remaining pages in this chapter before next week's group meeting.

Verses to Memorize and Meditate On

"In the beginning was the Word, and the Word was with God, and the Word was God." (John 1:1)

"He was in the beginning with God." (John 1:2)

"All things were made through him, and without him was not any thing made that was made." (John 1:3)

"And the Word became flesh and dwelt among us, and we have seen his glory, glory as of the only Son from the Father, full of grace and truth." (John 1:14)

"For God so loved the world, that he gave his only Son, that whoever believes in him should not perish but have eternal life." (John 3:16)

"For God did not send his Son into the world to condemn the world, but in order that the world might be saved through him." (John 3:17)

"Jesus said to her, 'Everyone who drinks of this water will be thirsty again, but whoever drinks of the water that I will give him will never be thirsty again.'" (John 4:13–14)

"But the testimony that I have is greater than that of John. For the works that the Father has given me to accomplish, the very works that I am doing, bear witness about me that the Father has sent me." (John 5:36)

"Jesus answered them, 'This is the work of God, that you believe in him whom he has sent.' " (John 6:29)

"Jesus said to them, 'I am the bread of life; whoever comes to me shall not hunger, and whoever believes in me shall never thirst.' " (John 6:35)

"Again Jesus spoke to them, saying, 'I am the light of the world. Whoever follows me will not walk in darkness, but will have the light of life.' " (John 8:12)

"Jesus said to her, 'I am the resurrection and the life. Whoever believes in me, though he die, yet shall he live, and everyone who lives and believes in me shall never die. Do you believe this?' " (John 11:25–26)

"Jesus said to him, 'I am the way, and the truth, and the life. No one comes to the Father except through me.' " (John 14:6)

"This is my commandment, that you love one another as I have loved you." (John 15:12)

"I have said these things to you, that in me you may have peace. In the world you will have tribulation. But take heart; I have overcome the world." (John 16:33)

"And this is eternal life, that they know you, the only true God, and Jesus Christ whom you have sent." (John 17:3)

"Then Pilate said to him, 'So you are a king?' Jesus answered, 'You say that I am a king. For this purpose I was born and for this purpose I have come into the world—to bear witness to the truth. Everyone who is of the truth listens to my voice.' " (John 18:37)

"When Jesus had received the sour wine, he said, 'It is finished,' and he bowed his head and gave up his spirit." (John 19:30)

"Jesus said to them again, 'Peace be with you. As the Father has sent me, even so I am sending you.' " (John 20:21)

"And after saying this he said to him, 'Follow me.' " (John 21:19)

1. The verse(s) I have chosen to memorize this week are:

_____

_____

_____

_____

_____

2. The method(s) I used to memorize are:

_____

_____

3. List which memorization method was most helpful and why:

_____

_____

_____

_____

4. List which memorization method was least helpful and why:

_____

_____

_____

_____

_____

5. Pick one or more verses, answer the questions below, and apply the verses to the meditation methods on the following page.

6. The verse(s) that I have chosen to meditate on are:

_____

_____

_____

_____

7. List which meditation method was most helpful and why:

_____
_____
_____
_____

8. List which meditation method was least helpful and why:

_____
_____
_____
_____

Meditation Method 1

1. Write the verse first, and then write it out in your own words.

_____
_____
_____
_____
_____
_____
_____
_____
_____
_____
_____
_____
_____
_____
_____
_____
_____
_____

Meditation Method 2

Examine the verse by answering the following questions:

1. What is the verse?

_____

2. Who wrote it?

_____

3. Who were they writing it to?

_____
_____
_____

4. When was it written?

_____
_____

5. What was their purpose in writing it?

_____
_____
_____
_____
_____

6. What else did you learn from this verse?

_____
_____
_____
_____
_____
_____

Meditation Method 3

Apply the verse to your own life by answering the following questions:

1. What is the verse?

_____

2. Explain a time in your life that this verse would have been helpful:

_____
_____
_____
_____
_____
_____
_____
_____
_____

3. How can I apply this verse to my daily life for the purpose of growing closer to the Lord?

_____
_____
_____
_____
_____
_____
_____
_____
_____

Week 4

Prayer and Worship

† Allow each person in the group to recite a Bible verse that they were able to memorize. In addition to this, discuss the favorite methods that were used in Scripture memorization and meditation.

† As a Group, discuss what you learned from last week's Bible reading.

✓ Is prayer a daily part of your life?

_____
_____
_____
_____

✓ If yes, do you have a set time that you pray each day?

_____
_____
_____
_____

✓ What does your prayer life look like?

_____

_____

_____

_____

✓ How would you like to improve your prayer life?

_____

_____

_____

_____

Our focus this week will be not only on developing a prayer time in our day but also on living our lives in an attitude of ceaseless prayer and adoration toward the Father.

The Bible tells us in 1 Thessalonians 5:16–18 that we should "rejoice always, pray without ceasing, give thanks in all circumstances." Worship and prayer go hand in hand. As we approach God in prayer, we should always acknowledge who He is as well as express His magnificence. Therefore, worship and adoration become the first part of our prayer. It puts our heart in awe of Him and who He is. Worship can be done at any time in any place. We outwardly express our worship when we openly praise Him with our voices in words or songs. On the other hand, inward worship is more an attitude and posture of our hearts as we meditate on who God is.

The ACTS prayer model is the method that is used in the _Growing in God_ journal. With this prayer method, we first worship our Creator; next we confess our sins and ask forgiveness; then, we thank Him for all that He has done in our lives; lastly, we bring our supplications or requests to Him as well as ask for His provisions and direction for our lives and the lives of others.

ACTS Prayer Model

Adoration: Praise and worship the Lord, proclaiming who He is. Here you can pray back Scriptures that speak of His characteristics and goodness, or you can simply pray from your heart and offer praise to Him.

Confession: We should reflect on our days, searching for areas in which our lives are not aligned with His Word, and then ask that He forgive us for our sins and wrongdoings.

Thanksgiving: Thank God for everything He has done for you.

Supplication: In supplication, we go to God for help and direction for ourselves and others. Nothing is too big or too small to take to our Father, and this is the time to do so.

✓ Have you ever used the ACTS prayer model during your time of prayer?

_____

_____

✓ List any other prayer methods that you have used:

_____

_____

_____

_____

✓ What do you think of when you hear the word *worship*?

_____

_____

_____

_____

✓ What does worship look like in your life?

_____

_____

_____

_____

✓ Are there ways in which you would like to improve your times of worship and adoration of God?

_____

_____

_____

_____

✓ Have you ever prayed Scripture back to God as worship to Him?

_____

_____

_____

_____

Sample Scriptures to Pray Back to God and Worship Him:

"The LORD is my strength and my song, and he has become my salvation; this is my God, and I will praise him, my father's God, and I will exalt him." (Exodus 15:2)

"Oh give thanks to the LORD, for he is good, for his steadfast love endures forever!" (Psalm 107:7)

"You have turned for me my mourning into dancing; you have loosed my sackcloth and clothed me with gladness, that my glory may sing your praise and not be silent. O LORD my God, I will give thanks to you forever!" (Psalm 30:11–12)

"I love you, O LORD, my strength. The LORD is my rock and my fortress and my deliverer, my God, my rock, in whom I take refuge, my shield, and the horn of my salvation, my stronghold. I call upon the LORD, who is worthy to be praised, and I am saved from my enemies." (Psalm 18:1–3)

Example of how to pray this verse back to God:

I love You, Lord, and I praise You today because You are my strength, my rock, my fortress, and my deliverer. You are my shield and the horn of my salvation. I praise You today because You are worthy. Amen.

Application

In the past couple weeks, you have learned to implement Bible study as well as Scripture memorization and meditation into your day. This week, we will be adding a daily prayer time as well consciously keeping our hearts and minds in a state of prayer and worship. I would encourage you to allow prayer as part of the very first moments of your day.

Complete Before Week 5 Meeting

☐ Read pages 23–25 in your *Growing in God* journal. (Pages 27-30 if you are using the teen edition)

☐ Establish a daily prayer time and begin to implement prayer into your daily life.

☐ Begin using your *Growing in God* book to journal your prayers. There is a blank page for each day of the year.

☐ If you have memorized a verse, pick another one to begin memorizing and follow the same steps in your *Growing in God* book as you did last week.

☐ Choose a verse to meditate on.

☐ Read week 3, days 1–7 in your Bible reading plan and record it in your *Growing in God* book.

☐ Complete the remaining pages in this chapter before next week's meeting.

☐ Be prepared to discuss your Bible reading, Scripture memorization, and prayer time during next week's meeting.

1. Look through your Bible, find some verses of praise, and write them out:

_____

_____

_____

_____

_____

_____

_____

_____

_____

_____

_____

_____

_____

_____

2. Pick three of those verses and write them out as prayers.

Verse 1: _____

_____

_____

_____

Verse 2: _____

_____

_____

Verse 3: _____

_____

_____

_____

3. Write out a Prayer using the ACTS prayer model:

Adoration (Praise):

_____
_____
_____
_____
_____
_____
_____

Confession:

_____
_____
_____
_____
_____
_____
_____

Give Thanks:

_____
_____
_____
_____
_____
_____
_____

Supplication (Requests):

_____
_____
_____
_____
_____
_____
_____

Week 5

Evangelism

† As a group, discuss what you learned from last week's Bible reading.

† Allow people to recite verses they have memorized.

† Allow a few people the opportunity to share their prayer journal page out loud if they feel comfortable doing so.

✓ Do you have a full understanding of the Gospel?

✓ Have you ever shared the Gospel with someone?

✓ If yes, what was the outcome and how did you feel about the encounter?

√ If no, what are your reasons for not sharing?

_____

_____

_____

So far during this study, you should have begun to add Bible study, Scripture memorization and meditation, and prayer and worship to your day. During these weeks, these disciplines have primarily been between only you and God. My prayer is that this time spent with Christ has already begun to help you grow closer to Him. Whether you realize it or not, these past several weeks have prepared you for this week. After Jesus' death on the cross, His burial, and His resurrection, He appeared to the eleven apostles with a command that would give direction and purpose to them for the remainder of their lives. This verse should be the driving force and motivation for this coming week. Just as Jesus spoke these words to the Eleven, so He also instructs the same to each of His followers.

"And Jesus came and said to them, "All authority in heaven and on earth has been given to me. Go therefore and make disciples of all nations, baptizing them in the name of the Father and of the Son and of the Holy Spirit, teaching them to observe all that I have commanded you. And behold, I am with you always, to the end of the age." (Matthew 28:18–20)

✓ If you have shared the Gospel before, did you follow a specific presentation or method?

_____

_____

_____

_____

_____

_____

_____

✓ Do you feel that your encounter sharing the Gospel was successful even if the person did not accept salvation in Christ at that moment?

_____

_____

_____

_____

_____

_____

_____

_____

The Gospel

It is important that we never assume someone has clarity or understanding of the truths of the Bible. Therefore, before I go any further, I find it necessary to lay out a quick but clear picture of the Gospel.

- God created the entire world and everything in it in six days.

- Sin entered the world through the first man and woman of creation. That sin nature exists in every person that has been born since then.

- God is Holy and cannot look upon sin; therefore, our sin separates us from Him.

- God had a plan from the very beginning to bring His people back into a right relationship with Him.

- God sent His Son, Jesus, who willingly stepped down from heaven to be born to a virgin named Mary.

- Jesus lived a perfect, sinless life and spent His time on earth teaching the truth of salvation.

- Jesus was sentenced to an undeserved but expected death. Here He became the ultimate sacrifice. He took on the sins of the whole world and offered forgiveness for them in return.

- His death gave us the opportunity to repent of those sins, accept Him as our Savior, and enter into a right relationship with a Holy God.

- On the third day after His death and burial, Jesus was resurrected into Heaven where He has prepared a place for all who have received Salvation in Him.

- This relationship offers us the promise of eternity spent with Him in heaven when our life on earth ends.

Understanding Evangelism and Our Roles in It

"I planted, Apollos watered, but God gave the growth." (1 Corinthians 3:6)

- It is the duty of every Christian to participate in evangelism, not just the pastors and teachers.

- Once you have a clear understanding of the Gospel and you have accepted salvation for yourself, it is time to share that same knowledge with others.

- Just because someone doesn't receive Christ at that moment does not mean that your efforts were unsuccessful.

- Our purpose in sharing the Gospel is to help someone grow in their knowledge and understanding and then allow God to do the rest.

- As Christians, we should pray for opportunities to share the Gospel with unbelievers.

- It is out of our control if or when someone chooses to receive Christ as their Lord and Savior; however, it is not out of our control if they hear it or not.

- You may never get the opportunity tomorrow that you have today. Make the most of those moments.

- It is not our job to save someone; God does that.

✓ List any other points that you would like to remind yourself of in the future:

_____
_____
_____
_____

Types of Evangelism

There are many ways in which we may have evangelism encounters. It was my assumption for years that it was always a one-on-one conversation in which one person shared Christ with another. And while that is one way, there are several others as well.

In person, one-on-one evangelism: The Gospel of Jesus Christ is shared by a believer to a non-believer for the purpose of deepening their knowledge and understanding of God and what it means to be a Christian.

Internet evangelism: Communicating the Gospel through the Internet via emails, texts, blogs, podcasts, and more.

Lifestyle evangelism: Living your life in a manner holy and pleasing to God so that unbelievers see the evidence of Christ living in you. You then work to intentionally build relationships with others, and over time you are given opportunities to share with them.

✓ These are just a few. List some other options that you are aware of:

_____
_____
_____
_____

✓ If you have ever shared the Gospel, which type or types have you used?

_____
_____
_____
_____

✓ Which feels the most comfortable, and why?

_____
_____
_____
_____

✓ Which feels the least comfortable, and why?

_____
_____
_____
_____

Gospel Presentations

Gospel presentation are full presentations of the basic truths of who Jesus is, concerning His life, His purpose, and His death, burial, and resurrection, followed by a brief explanation of why we need Him and the steps one takes to receive salvation. Lastly, the presentation finishes with the promise of spending eternity with Him in heaven.

✓ List Gospel presentations or ways to share the Gospel that you are aware of:

_____

_____

✓ Have you ever used a Gospel presentation for evangelism? If yes, explain.

_____

_____

_____

_____

✓ What was the outcome?

_____

_____

_____

_____

✓ If you could go back to that moment and do it again, what, if anything, would you do differently?

_____

_____

_____

_____

The Romans Road to Salvation

The "Romans Road" is a compilation of verses from the Book of Romans. These verses give a clear explanation of God's plan of salvation, and they are a wonderful tool to use to share God's love with an unbeliever.

- **As humans, we all have sinned.**
  "For all have sinned and fall short of the glory of God" (Romans 3:23).

- **Sin has consequences.**
  "For the wages of sin is death" (Romans 6:23).

- **The free gift of God is life.**
  "But the free gift of God is eternal life in Christ Jesus our Lord"   (Romans 6:23).
  "But God shows his love for us in that while we were still sinners, Christ died for us" (Romans 5:8).

- **We confess Jesus is Lord.**
  "Because, if you confess with your mouth that Jesus is Lord and believe in your heart that God raised him from the dead, you will be saved. For with the heart one believes and is justified, and with the mouth one confesses and is saved" (Romans 10:9–10).

- **We have assurance of salvation.**
  "Everyone who calls on the name of the Lord will be saved" (Romans 10:13).

Application

This week, you will be implementing your sixth discipline. But first, spend some time in prayer asking that God would arrange encounters with people that need to hear about how to receive salvation in Christ. Next, pray for wisdom and boldness as He places people in front of you. Sharing Christ with those around you can be a little uncomfortable and even a little nerve-wracking. But I want to encourage you to push through those feelings and remember that as believers, this is our purpose and responsibility.

Complete Before Week 6 Meeting

☐ Read pages 26–29 in your *Growing in God* journal (pages 31-38 if you are using the teen edition).

☐ Pray daily for the lost souls who need to hear the Gospel.

☐ As God brings people to your heart and mind, write their names on the bottom of that month's accountability page.

☐ Continue meditating and memorizing Bible verses.

☐ Read week 4, days 1–7 in your Bible reading plan, and record it in your *Growing in God* journal.

☐ Continue journaling your prayers in your *Growing in God* book.

☐ Share the Gospel with at least one person this week.

☐ Complete the remaining pages in this chapter before next week's meeting.

☐ Share your evangelism experience with the group next week. Remember, it is important that we keep confidential what needs to be kept confidential regarding others.

1. This is the method I have chosen to use this week to present the Gospel to someone:

_____

_____

(It is fine to have more than one method, and it's also good to have a plan, but be willing to change routes as God speaks to you in each individual situation.)

2. Write about your Gospel-sharing encounter:

_____

_____

_____

_____

_____

3. What do you wish you would have said or done differently?

_____

_____

_____

_____

4. How will this help you moving forward?

_____

_____

_____

_____

5. How would you rate your stewardship of the gospel in this evangelism encounter?

_____

_____

_____

_____

Week 6

Solitude and Fasting

† As a group, discuss things that you learned from last week's Bible study.

† Recite verses that you memorized last week.

† Discuss your Gospel encounters with your group.

✓ Do you set aside quiet time in your day for the sole purpose of giving God your undivided time and attention?

_____
_____
_____
_____
_____

✓ If yes, how has this helped you to grow in your walk?

_____
_____
_____
_____
_____

This week, we are going to explore the discipline of solitude and how it can help us grow closer to Christ and open our eyes to see the plan He has laid out before us. We will also briefly cover fasting and what that looks like for believers and followers of Christ.

Solitude

Quiet time seems almost impossible to find in the busy world that we live in. I can promise you that it doesn't come easy, and it most definitely takes intentionality on our part. The purpose of this discipline is to create a space in which we can give God our complete, undivided attention. In this place, He will open our hearts to hear from Him as we seek His perfect will for our lives. When I feel completely overwhelmed with life, I step away as much as possible. Sometimes it's for an hour, and sometimes it's for a day.

Tips on Practicing Solitude

- Be intentional in your scheduling. Schedule a time when you can free your mind from the daily duties and things that are waiting to be accomplished.

- Set aside a specific amount of time. Try beginning with thirty minutes unless you feel that the Lord is calling you to more. Just sit and be with God during that time.

- Let your family or other people most likely to contact you know that you will be unavailable during that time. This will free your mind from worrying that someone is trying to get in touch with you or that someone may be worried about you.

- Find a calm, relaxing place where you are not likely to be interrupted. For some, it's beside water or a stream; for others, on a mountain; for still others, it's just a quiet room of their house. I tend to go toward nature because I enjoy sitting and looking at the beauty of His creation.

- Pray. I sit and pray about whatever it is that comes to my mind and my heart.

- Recite Scripture that you have memorized.

- Meditate on Scripture and who God is. Allow your heart to rest on the goodness of God.

- As you implement solitude, continue to add to the thirty minutes.

- Imagine that God is sitting right beside you and that you are just resting in Him.

✓ List other things that come to your mind regarding the discipline of solitude and ways that you can make it an addition to your relationship with Christ:

_____
_____
_____
_____
_____
_____
_____
_____

Fasting

Fasting for the purpose of growing in God is a powerful tool designed only for believers and followers of Christ. It shows our dependence on Him to provide for our lives spiritually, mentally, and physically. Fasting and solitude work in combination together. Fasting encourages another aspect of giving God our complete, undivided attention. It is something that I do in my private walk with Christ. I commit my time to praying over specific needs that have been placed on my heart as I intentionally abstain from food for a specific amount of time to depend on and focus on Him completely. This time is designed to be between you and the Lord. My encouragement for you with this discipline is that you gain a total and complete understanding of what biblical fasting means and what the purposes of it are before rendering it a part of your journey to grow in

God. A brief explanation is included in the *Growing in God* book. If you are looking for additional knowledge and readings, I would encourage you to read the fasting section in *Spiritual Disciplines for the Christian Life* by Donald Whitney.

✓ Do you have a complete understanding of biblical fasting?

_____

_____

_____

✓ Have you ever entered a biblical fast for the purpose of growth in God?

_____

_____

_____

✓ If you don't have a complete understanding of fasting, list some tangible steps that you can take to increase your knowledge on the matter:

_____

_____

_____

_____

✓ Take some time to share as a group about your understanding of fasting and tips to help you gain a deeper understanding of it:

_____

_____

_____

_____

_____

Together as group, read the following verses in the Bible regarding biblical fasting.

- Matthew 4:1–11
- Matthew 6:16–18
- Luke 4:1–4

Application

Over the period of this study, we have covered eight spiritual disciplines: Bible study, memorization, meditation, prayer, worship, evangelism, solitude, and fasting. These have been introduced one at a time so that you could understand each one individually before putting all of it together. This coming week is when you put it all together. If there is one discipline (or a few) that you are struggling to implement, I suggest temporarily removing it as you work on the others, and add it back slowly. Use your *Growing in God* journal to write down all your prayers, Bible studies, and other disciplines. At the end of one year, how amazing it will be to see the goodness of God written and evident all throughout your book!

Complete Before Week 7 Meeting

☐ Begin to make all the disciplines a part of your daily life. Some of them may not be applicable every day. For instance, I would say that most people do not fast every day. In addition to this, solitude may not happen every day. If God calls you to this, then that's wonderful, but if not, focus on the other disciplines daily through the strength and power of the Lord.

☐ Read week 5, days 1–7 in your Bible reading plan. Remember to use the Notes section in the back of your *Growing in God* book to record your notes from your daily readings.

☐ When you have successfully memorized a verse, remember to write it in the back of your *Growing in God* book so that you can review it from time to time.

☐ Complete the remaining pages in this chapter before next week's meeting.

☐ Intentionally plan a time of solitude once during this coming week.

☐ Take some time to educate yourself more on biblical fasting by reading what the Bible says about it and how Jesus taught it to His disciples.

1. Which discipline have you found to be the most encouraging in your daily walk with God, and why?

_____
_____
_____
_____
_____

2. Which one has been the most difficult to incorporate or understand, and why?

_____
_____
_____
_____

3. What can help you to be consistent with the addition of spiritual disciplines into your day?

_____
_____
_____
_____

4. What does accountability from other believers look like in your life?

_____
_____
_____
_____

5. How important is accountability from other believers to you?

_____
_____
_____

Week 7

Accountability

† As a group, discuss what you learned from last week's Bible reading.

† Allow individuals to recite verses they have memorized.

† As a group, discuss your answers from the homework on page 66 in this chapter.

† Discuss with one another your experiences in solitude.

As believers, it is imperative that we seek and find accountability. We need to be surrounded with others who are devoted and committed to the ways of the Lord.

Read the verses below together as a group:

"Therefore, confess your sins to one another and pray for one another, that you may be healed. The prayer of a righteous person has great power as it is working." (James 5:16)

"Therefore encourage one another and build one another up, just as you are doing." (1 Thessalonians 5:11)

"And let us consider how to stir up one another to love and good works, not neglecting to meet together, as is the habit of some, but encouraging one another, and all the more as you see the Day drawing near." (Hebrews 10:24–25)

"Iron sharpens iron, and one man sharpens another." (Proverbs 27:17)

Accountability Challenge

In your group meeting, your leader will randomly pair you up with an accountability partner. The purpose in this relationship is to strengthen, help, and encourage each other as you continue to implement disciplines. Below you will find some tips to help you move forward with your accountability partner. We all have different levels of time and capacity to accommodate these relationships, and it may look different to each of you.

- If you have minimal extra time, commit to some form of communication with the person once a week. This may be over email, in a phone call, or by text.

- Maybe you have gaps of extra time available to meet for coffee or lunch. If this is the case, meet in person weekly and offer support and encouragement to each other.

- For those who are looking to continue a one-on-one study, commit to another Bible plan that you can study together. Recite Scripture memory verses to each other.

✓ What are other ways to add time with an accountability partner to your weeks?

_____
_____
_____
_____
_____
_____
_____
_____
_____
_____
_____
_____

After partners are selected, allow them the rest of the meeting to discuss together and come up with a plan outlining what this will look like for them.

My Accountability Partner

My accountability partner: _____

Our plan to hold one another accountable is:

_____
_____
_____
_____
_____
_____
_____
_____
_____
_____
_____
_____
_____
_____
_____
_____

We believe that this is important to our growth in God because:

_____
_____
_____
_____
_____
_____
_____
_____
_____
_____
_____
_____
_____
_____

Next Steps

I pray that you all have enjoyed this study as much as I enjoyed creating it. You have one more week of the Bible reading plan to complete. It was designed for you complete it after the study is finished so that you can use this last week of reading from the Book of John to discuss with your accountability partner. Commit yourselves to continuing your plan with your partner as you work on implementing these eight disciplines into your day.

If you are looking for additional resources such as weekly Bible reading plans and Scripture memory challenges, visit www.joyfullyhis.org and subscribe to receive these resources weekly via email.

Joyfully HIS,

Jennifer N. Pearson

Understanding Salvation

How to receive God's free gift of salvation:

1. Understand your need for a Savior.

2. Recognize that God is exactly who He says He is.

3. Understand that through His Son, Jesus, you can be saved.

4. Confess your sins.

5. Repent (turn away) from your sins and your old way of life.

6. Walk in assurance, knowing that you have been forgiven and that a new life in Christ awaits you.

Prayer of Salvation

Dear God,
Today I recognize my need for You in my
life and proclaim the truth that apart from
You, I can do nothing. I humble myself
before You and confess to You that I am
a sinner and in need of Your grace. I
believe that You are the one, true God and
that You sent Your one and only Son to
die on the cross to save me from my sins.
I believe that because of this I can have
eternal life with You. I ask You now that
You would cleanse me from these sins and
create in me a clean heart. From this day
forward I want to live my life solely for
You as my Lord. Thank You for hearing my
prayers, saving my soul, and making me a
new creation.
Amen.

Made in the USA
Columbia, SC
17 April 2023

15500458R00043